# IDA B. WELLS-BARNETT

## and the Antilynching Crusade

by Suzanne Freedman

GATEWAY CIVIL RIGHTS
THE MILLBROOK PRESS
BROOKFIELD, CONNECTICUT

*To Sally Anne, Hannah Caitlin, and Erik Michael*

Photographs courtesy of Department of Special Collections, The University of Chicago Library: cover inset, pp. ▮▮, ▮, 9, 20, 27, 29; UPI/Bettmann: cover background, pp. 2–3; Bettmann Archive: pp. 6, 11, 22, 25; Mississippi Department of Archives and History, Archives and Library Division: p. 8; Memphis Shelby County Public Library & Information Center: p. 13; Schomburg Center for Research in Black Culture, New York Public Library: pp. 15, 18; Chicago Historical Society: p. 17; NAACP National Public Relations Department: p. 24; National Park Service: p. 30.

Library of Congress Cataloging-in-Publication Data
Freedman, Suzanne, 1932–
Ida B. Wells-Barnett and the antilynching crusade
by Suzanne Freedman.
p.   cm. — (Gateway civil rights)
Includes bibliographical references and index.
Summary: Traces the life of the journalist, focusing on her lifelong fight to stop lynching and to bring the nation's attention to the injustices suffered by blacks.
ISBN 1-56294-377-4 (lib. bdg.)
1. Wells-Barnett, Ida B., 1862–1931—Juvenile literature. 2. Civil rights workers—United States—Biography—Juvenile literature.  3. Journalists—United States—Biography. 4. United States—Race relations—Juvenile literature. 5. Afro-Americans—Social conditions—Juvenile literature. [1. Wells-Barnett, Ida B., 1862–1931. 2. Journalists. 3. Civil rights workers. 4. Afro-Americans—Biography. 5. Race relations.] I. Title. II. Series.
E185.97.W55F74   1994
323′.092—dc20     [B]     92-45855  CIP  AC

Published by The Millbrook Press
2 Old New Milford Road, Brookfield, Connecticut 06804

IS THIS THE AMERICAN PRINCIPLE
America The Only Spot On Earth Where A Human Being May Be Burned At Stake.
The Failure Of The Anti Lynching Bill Will Be A Castastrophe For America

On March 8, 1892, three white men broke into the People's Grocery in Memphis, Tennessee. Its three black owners fired at the robbers in self-defense. When the police arrived, they arrested the owners and put them in jail.

Early the next morning at about 2 A.M., an angry mob of white men hustled store owners Thomas Moss, Calvin McDowell, and Henry Stewart out of jail. Hatless and shoeless, they were pushed into the switch engine of a train that was sitting on the tracks just behind the jail. The train took them one mile north of the Memphis city limits. At a prearranged time, the locomotive blew its whistle to deaden the sound of firing as the three men were brutally shot to death.

When Ida Bell Wells, editor and part owner of the Memphis *Free Speech,* heard about the incident, she was furious. The three young men had been her friends. She wrote an article in protest, saying, ''Thomas Moss was a favorite with everybody; yet he was murdered with no more consideration than if he had been a dog.''

In those days, lynchings—mob killings—were common in the South. For the most part, the mobs were white and the victims were black. White people did not wait for a trial to determine innocence or guilt. They took the law into their own hands, and most of the time white lawmakers let them get away with it.

*Ida B. Wells (left) poses with Betty Moss and her children. Betty's husband, Thomas, was murdered by a mob of nine white men.*

*During the year in which Ida Wells's friends were lynched,*
*a total of 230 such mob killings were reported.*

Ida Wells was determined to publish the truth. It took courage to speak out against lynching. That was a quality that Wells did not lack.

Three months later, while Wells was away on a trip to Philadelphia and New York City, she learned that some of the leading citizens of Memphis had wrecked the offices of the *Free Speech*. They left a note saying that if Wells tried to publish her newspaper again she would die. Her home was being watched; so were the trains to Memphis.

Wells knew that it would be foolish to go back. She had just met T. Thomas Fortune, coeditor of the black newspaper *New York Age*. He recognized her talent and courage. "Ida has plenty of nerve," he said; "she is smart as a steel trap and has a forceful personality."

Fortune offered her a job as a weekly writer with a partial interest in the *New York Age*. Ida Wells accepted on the spot. Now she had thousands of new readers to whom she could tell her story. Her antilynching crusade had begun!

## A Proud Struggle

Ida Bell Wells was born into slavery on July 16, 1862, in Holly Springs, Mississippi, during the second year of the Civil War. Fortunately, little fighting took place there. Some fine homes were wrecked and burned by Confederate soldiers, but all in all, Holly Springs was a peaceful place to live.

Ida's mother, Elizabeth Warrenton, known as Lizzie, had been born a slave in Virginia. She had come to Mississippi to work as a cook on the plantation of Mr. Bolling. She met Ida's father, Jim Wells, there. He and Lizzie first married as slaves and then remarried as free people after the Civil War brought an end to slavery in 1865.

*Slavery was abolished in 1865 with the North's victory over the South in the Civil War. But on some plantations, life did not change much.*

Jim, who had been trained as a carpenter when he was a slave, had no trouble finding work as a freeman. He even built a house for his family. He was interested in politics, too. "My earliest recollections are of reading the newspaper to my father and . . . his friends," Ida later recalled.

She learned to read the Bible, too. Since it was the only book that was allowed to be read in the Wellses' home on

Sundays, Ida read it over and over again. She became deeply religious.

During the week she went to the newly established Rust College school, where her father was a trustee. Her mother, Lizzie, showed a deep concern for her children's education and would often visit the school to check on their progress. She had nothing to worry about in Ida's case. Her teachers said she was "an exceedingly apt pupil."

Lizzie also taught her eight children how to do housework and gave each one a regular task to perform. This was fortunate, because a disaster would soon tear apart the happiness and order of the Wells family.

A yellow-fever epidemic hit Holly Springs in 1878. Many people died. Ida lost both of her parents and her baby brother, Stanley, as well. (Another brother had died a few years before.)

As the eldest of the remaining six children, Ida knew it was her duty to look after the family. She needed a job, so she let down her skirts and put up her hair to look older than her sixteen years. She got a job teaching at a local school for twenty-five dollars a month.

During the week, family friends and neighbors took care of the children while Ida rode a mule six miles every day to work. In the evening she cooked dinner, washed clothes, and prepared the children for the next day. On the weekend she saw that they had their Saturday-night bath and that shoes were shined and ready for Sunday church. Ida later wrote with confidence, "I was old enough to fend for myself."

## Leaving Holly Springs Behind

Five years later, after leaving the other three children with relatives, Ida and her sisters Annie and Lily moved into their Aunt Belle's house in Memphis, Tennessee. Memphis was only forty miles north of Holly Springs, so the other children could come to visit.

Ida found another teaching position there. She also began to study for a special exam that would enable her to teach in a city school for blacks and so bring in more money for the family. In the summer she took classes at Fisk University, a black college in Nashville, Tennessee.

One day, on May 4, 1884, twenty-two-year-old Ida was riding the Chesapeake and Ohio Railroad to a new teaching job in Woodstock, Tennessee. At that time, white women who were traveling alone usually sat in the ladies' coach. Black people, both men and women, were expected to ride in a different car than white people. Such separation, or segregation, of the races was one of the Jim Crow laws that had sprung up in the South after the Civil War. These discriminatory laws defined acceptable behavior for black people in public.

Ida took a seat in the ladies' car as she always did. The conductor asked her to move to the car reserved for blacks, which was also a smoking car. Ida refused. She said that she was in the ladies' car and intended to stay there. The conductor tried to drag her from her seat. Ida bit him on the back of his hand. She was then forced from the train. The train took off as she stood on the platform, furious and alone, the sleeves of her linen dress torn off.

Ida sued the railroad and won her case. The headlines in the December 25 edition of the Memphis *Daily Appeal* announced: "A Darky Damsel Obtains a Verdict for Damages Against the Railroad—What It Cost to Put a Colored School Teacher in a Smoking Car—Verdict for $500."

Ida Wells won her first battle for justice as a black person and a woman in America.

*A white man tells a black man to go to a separate railroad car. Segregation was lawful in many states for about one hundred years after the end of slavery.*

# "Princess
## of the Press"

Ida Wells loved to read. Her favorite writers were Charles Dickens and Louisa May Alcott. She also read all of William Shakespeare's plays. Wells joined a literary club that met every Friday afternoon at the local church. Members would recite poetry to each other while music played in the background. Meetings always closed with a reading by the editor of a journal called the *Evening Star*.

The journal included news items, literary notes, poetry, and a column about personalities called "They Say." When the journal's editor had to leave his job, Wells was asked to take his place.

Then one Friday the Reverend R. N. Countee, a Baptist minister, visited the literary club and invited Wells to write for his weekly religious newspaper, the *Living Way*. Although Wells felt uncertain of herself as a writer, she knew she was a keen observer of conditions in black schools and churches. She felt that people who had little or no education should be able to read about their concerns in plain, commonsense writing. "I never used a word of two syllables where one would serve the purpose," said Wells. She signed her articles "Iola."

People began to call her the "Princess of the Press." She had earned the title. Since her career on the *Living Way* began,

*The Beale Avenue Baptist Church, where the* Living Way *had its offices.*

she had started writing for newspapers in Detroit, Michigan; Kansas City, Missouri; and Little Rock, Arkansas, as well as for magazines, and daily and weekly newspapers in Tennessee. She wrote for the Memphis *Free Speech,* too.

She began to feel that it was time to run her own newspaper. The Reverend F. Nightingale and J. L. Fleming owned the *Free Speech* in 1889. Wells decided to buy an interest in it and become an equal partner. She became the editor, Fleming was the business manager, and Rev. Nightingale took charge of sales. (Five hundred copies were sold every Sunday in his Memphis church, the largest congregation in Tennessee.)

Things went smoothly for about two years, until Wells wrote some articles describing the poor conditions in Memphis black schools. There were not enough of them, the buildings were in terrible shape, and the quality of the teaching was not very good. Wells was still teaching at the time. She knew that she could lose her job if school board members found out that she had written these articles, so she did not sign them. But word leaked out, and she was fired.

*An 1893 portrait
of Ida B. Wells.*

Wells decided to try to make a living by writing full-time for the paper. She loved her work, and she worked hard. Within a year the paper's circulation increased from fifteen hundred to four thousand. The *Free Speech* had become an influential voice for black people. Wells's salary increased, too. Soon she was making within ten dollars of what she had made as a teacher.

Then came the lynching of her three friends. The whole course of Ida Wells's life changed once again.

## With Voice and Pen

Wells's article and the angry voice of the *Free Speech* echoed through town after the lynching. The paper advised blacks to leave Memphis, "which will neither protect our lives and property nor give us a fair trial in the courts . . . but murders us in cold blood." Hundreds of blacks headed west to start new lives.

Wells, too, looked for an escape. Long before the lynching, she had been invited to Philadelphia, Pennsylvania, to cover a church conference for her paper. She thought this might be a good time to consider the East as a possible place to live.

She left Memphis in the spring of 1892. After stopping in Philadelphia, she took the train to New York City. There she was greeted by the editor, T. Thomas Fortune, who told her, "From the rumpus you kicked up, I am afraid you'll have to stay in New York."

With the offices of the *Free Speech* destroyed and her career in Memphis at an end, Wells did not hesitate long. She decided to accept Fortune's offer to write for the *New York Age* and to make New York the base from which she would launch a career in public speaking.

*T. Thomas Fortune gave Wells a start in big-city publishing.*

She first spoke in New York City to an audience of women about the horrors of lynching. Wells was frightened. She had been a writer for many years, written essays in school, recited from memory, even made speeches asking for newspaper subscriptions. But this was the first time she had to deliver "an honest-to-goodness'' address. She wrote out every detail of the lynching in Memphis and read from that with tears streaming down her cheeks. The audience was moved.

She told her story in Boston and New Bedford, Massachusetts; in Providence and Newport, Rhode Island; and in New Haven, Connecticut. In 1893 and 1894, Wells traveled to England, Scotland, and Ireland, spreading the news about lynchings to audiences abroad. She told people that over one thousand blacks had been murdered by mobs in the past ten years, and that ninety-three black men and women had already been lynched in 1893.

''I come to England and ask her to . . . speak out against this . . . 'National Crime' and put a stop to it,'' said Wells. The British were horrified, and news about these racial killings spread.

Upon her return from her first trip abroad, Wells went to the opening of the Chicago World's Columbian Exposition. She met with her friend the famous black leader, writer, and former minister to Haiti Frederick Douglass. He was presiding over the Haitian pavilion. When Wells discovered that this was the only place where blacks were allowed to participate, she published a pamphlet in protest. Douglass wrote the introduction and then gave Wells a desk where she sat and handed out copies to the public.

*The opening day ceremony at the Chicago World's Columbian Exposition. Wells worked with Frederick Douglass at the Haitian pavilion, and the two became lifelong friends.*

Wells decided to make Chicago her home. She began working right away on the Chicago *Conservator*, the city's oldest black newspaper and one of the few that had always spoken out against lynching. But she had another reason for staying in Chicago. She had fallen in love with the founder of the *Conservator*, Ferdinand L. Barnett.

# THE BLACK WARRIOR

Ida Wells-Barnett first met Frederick Douglass in February 1893 when he heard her speak against lynching. They became fast friends and firm allies.

When Ida wrote her fiery article on the Memphis lynching in 1892, Douglass answered, "Brave woman! You have done your people and mine a service. If the American conscience were only half alive . . . a scream of horror, shame and indignation would rise to heaven. . . . What a revelation of existing conditions your writing has been for me."

Despite the difference in their ages (Douglass was forty-five years older), they were remarkably alike. Both began their careers writing about injustices to blacks. Both loved to dress well and were scornful of those who did not "keep their socks pulled up." And both were editors and eloquent speakers.

In November 1894, Wells-Barnett and Douglass were the main speakers at a meeting in Providence, Rhode Island. As they waited to be introduced, Douglass asked Wells-Barnett if she was nervous. Ida replied, "No. I am only a mouthpiece through which to tell the story of lynching. . . . I have told it so often . . . it makes its own way."

Ida never saw Frederick Douglass again. He died three months later. At his memorial service, Ida said, "We lost the greatest man the Negro race has ever produced."

The two were married on June 27, 1895. Ida was thirty-three years old. Years later the poet Langston Hughes would say of their union: "Ida B. Wells married another crusader and together they continued their campaign for equal rights for Negro Americans."

Wells, now Wells-Barnett, had already bought the *Conservator* from Barnett and his partners before their marriage. On the Monday following the ceremony, she walked into the office and took charge.

The couple's first son, Charles Aked, was born in 1896. Six months later, she took him on a speaking tour across the state of Illinois. She said, "I am the only woman in the country with a nursing baby to make political speeches."

*Ferdinand Barnett, about twelve years after his marriage to Ida B. Wells.*

But when a second son, Herman Kohlsaat, was born one year later, Ida gave up her active life for the time being. "Motherhood is a profession just like schoolteaching and lecturing," she said, "and once I am launched on such a career, I owe it to myself to become as expert as possible in the practice of that profession."

The Barnetts had two more children. Ida was a kind and loving mother, but she was also very firm. A large, handsome woman, all she had to do was direct her powerful, flashing eyes at her children when they were out of control and they would stop dead in their tracks. Fiercely protective of her family, she kept a pistol in the house and dared anyone to cross her threshold to harm them.

Soon, though, Ida Wells-Barnett would be off to defend more than her home. Another man had been lynched in the South.

*Ida Wells-Barnett with her four children in 1909. She managed to juggle family life with her ongoing battle to end the crime of lynching.*

## "The Backbone
## of Mrs. Barnett"

In the spring of 1898, in Anderson, South Carolina, Frazier Baker had been appointed postmaster of the town. The whites did not want this black man to have the job. A mob of about four hundred people gathered outside Baker's house and set it on fire. Members of his family were shot as they tried to escape the flames. Frazier Baker was left to die inside the burning house.

When Ida Wells-Barnett heard about the incident, she put her domestic routines aside. She led a delegation of black Chicago citizens to Washington, D.C., to urge President William McKinley to act. Wells-Barnett told the president, "Nowhere in the civilized world do men go out . . . to hunt down, shoot, hang or burn to death a single individual unarmed and . . . powerless."

McKinley listened. Then he told her that he would send Secret Service agents to Anderson to arrest the lynchers. Her trip had not been in vain.

Another lynching took place in December 1909. This time it was much closer to home. Sheriff Frank Davis of Cairo, Illinois, arrested "Frog" James, a poor black man. He was falsely accused of murdering a local white woman. Davis and his deputy took James to the railroad depot, where they boarded

*Masked horsemen ride away
from a hanging.*

a train headed for the woods outside of town. When the train came to a halt, an angry mob of white men dragged Frog from the train. They hanged him and then shot him with hundreds of bullets.

Ida Wells-Barnett lost no time in going to Cairo to learn the facts. The people of Cairo knew her reputation as an antilynching crusader. They asked her to plead with the governor for them. Sheriff Davis had been temporarily suspended from office; they wanted to be rid of him for good.

Wells-Barnett rode two hundred miles by train to the Illinois capital, Springfield, to see Governor Charles Deneen. "The state of Illinois has had too many terrible lynchings," she told him. "If this man is reinstated, it will simply mean an increase of lynchings in the state of Illinois and an encouragement to mob violence.''

After considering her words, the governor announced that Sheriff Davis would have to turn in his badge because he had not properly protected prisoner Frog James. ''Lynching should have no place in Illinois,'' the governor concluded.

In its January 1, 1909, edition, the Chicago *Defender* covered the Cairo investigation. ''If we only had a few men with the backbone of Mrs. Barnett,'' it declared, ''lynching would soon come to a halt in America.''

## Political Power

Back in 1893, Wells-Barnett had created the Ida B. Wells Club, the first civic club for black women. Then, in February 1909, she formed the National Negro Conference. Its purpose was to further the cause of justice for black people. That same year, she also took part in the Niagara Meeting, which led to the founding of the National Association for the Advancement of Colored People (NAACP)—the most powerful civil rights organization in America today. Wells-Barnett worked with the NAACP to help stop the violent acts of such hate groups as the Ku Klux Klan.

*This Silent March on Washington, D.C., in 1917, was the first organized protest against lynching. The renowned scholar and activist W.E.B. Du Bois played a drum (second from the right).*

Wells-Barnett's driving commitment to equal rights did not stop there. She had been a member of the Women's Suffrage Association as long as she had lived in Chicago. Except in a few states, women would not be allowed to vote in national elections until 1920.

## POWER OF THE BALLOT

In Ida Wells-Barnett's day the right to vote, or suffrage, was limited. After the end of the Civil War, the Fourteenth Amendment to the U.S. Constitution, ratified in 1868, allowed newly freed black men the right to vote but not the women—white and black alike—who had helped to win the war. A woman's right to vote was left up to individual states.

By 1896, Colorado, Wyoming, Utah, and Idaho had granted women the right to vote in national elections. But in other states, women could vote only in state or local elections. In some states, women could not vote at all.

Ida Wells-Barnett fought hard for women's suffrage. In 1916 she and five thousand other suffragists marched in torrential rain to demand a voice at the Republican National Convention.

Finally, in 1920, the Constitution's Nineteenth Amendment was ratified. It stated: "The right of citizens of the United States to vote shall not be denied . . . by the United States or by any state on account of sex."

*A suffragette parade in New York, 1912.*

Wells-Barnett organized her own club for black women, in 1913, calling it the Alpha Suffrage Club. When women in Illinois were granted the right to vote, in 1914, she showed members how to use their votes to their advantage. The club's goal was to get black women to register so they could put the first black man on the city council or perhaps elect the first black mayor one day.

At first the women were discouraged. They did not think this was possible. But they listened carefully to what the black candidates had to say. Then, for the first time, they voted. With support from the Alpha Suffrage Club, Oscar DePriest, a black man, won a seat on the city council. And William Hale Thompson, a white man, was elected mayor of Chicago with the largest number of black votes ever!

## A Run for Office

Ida Wells-Barnett kept on fighting injustice and discrimination all over the United States. Whenever there were reports of race riots, she acted. She would appeal to civil rights groups, newspapers, mass church meetings—anywhere she could find people to listen. She would raise money by asking friends and organizations to donate funds or by selling subscriptions to the Chicago *Defender*. She would travel to the riot scene, make her investigation, and return to Chicago to report the facts.

She joined the Metropolitan Community Church at its founding in 1920. As president of its Sunday Forum, she brought in outstanding speakers and led discussions about religious, civic and social issues. In 1928 she began to write about her thirty-six-year struggle to put an end to lynching. It was not until 1970, though, that her daughter edited her memoirs and had them published. The book was called *Crusade for Justice*.

In 1930, Ida Wells-Barnett ran for a seat in the Illinois Senate. Her opponent was a black state legislator named Adelbert H. Roberts. She worked hard to win. Five hundred people signed a petition to place her name on the ballot. Wells-Barnett distributed cards and letters and posted ads in windows.

Despite her efforts, she lost. Adelbert Roberts got 6,604 votes; Ida Wells-Barnett got only 585. She was

*Ida with Ferdinand and daughter Alfreda in 1919.*

very disappointed. But she had proved that a qualified black woman could run for public office. She hoped that one day she could try again and be elected.

## The End of
## the Fight

Unhappily, she never had the chance. On the Monday following the first day of spring in 1931, Ida B. Wells-Barnett got sick. She was rushed, unconscious, to the nearest hospital. She died on March 25, the thirty-fifth birthday of her oldest son, Charles. She was sixty-nine years old.

Her memory lives on in many ways. In 1950, Chicago named her one of its outstanding women. A housing project there bears her name, and the family home, the Ida B. Wells-Barnett house, became a national historic landmark in 1974. In February 1990 a U.S. postage stamp was issued in her honor to celebrate Black History Month.

Ida B. Wells-Barnett has been described as courageous and determined. She was a fiery reformer and feminist. Neither her marriage nor the raising of her four children kept her from acting on her beliefs. Wells-Barnett—she surrendered nothing, not even her name—will be remembered for her fight against lynching and her passionate demand for justice.

# IMPORTANT EVENTS IN THE LIFE OF IDA B. WELLS-BARNETT

| | |
|---|---|
| 1862 | Ida Bell Wells is born on July 16 in Holly Springs, Mississippi. |
| 1878 | Ida's parents and brother die in a yellow-fever epidemic. |
| 1884 | Ida successfully sues the Chesapeake and Ohio Railroad. |
| 1889 | Ida becomes part owner of the Memphis *Free Speech*. |
| 1892 | Three of Ida's friends are lynched. Her antilynching crusade begins. |
| 1893–1894 | Wells travels to England, Scotland, and Ireland to tell the story of lynching. |
| 1895 | Ida Wells marries Ferdinand L. Barnett on June 27. She makes Chicago, Illinois, her home. |
| 1909 | Wells-Barnett participates in the founding of the National Association for the Advancement of Colored People (NAACP). |
| 1913 | Wells-Barnett founds the Alpha Suffrage Club to press for voting rights for women. |
| 1931 | Ida Bell Wells-Barnett dies on March 25 in Chicago. |

# FIND OUT MORE ABOUT IDA B. WELLS-BARNETT AND HER TIMES

Books: *The Civil Rights Movement in America from 1865 to the Present* by Patricia McKissack and Fredrick McKissack (Chicago: Childrens Press, 1987).

*Frederick Douglass and the War Against Slavery* by Evelyn Bennett (Brookfield, Conn.: The Millbrook Press, 1993).

*Ida B. Wells-Barnett: A Voice Against Violence* by Patricia McKissack and Fredrick McKissack (Hillside, N.J.: Enslow Publishers, 1991).

Places: The Ida B. Wells-Barnett house is located at 3624 South Martin Luther King, Jr., Drive, Chicago, Illinois.

# INDEX

Page numbers in *italics* refer to illustrations.